FIXED STARS

Fixed Stars © Marisa Siegel, 2022
Cover, Illustrations, & Design © Trisha Previte, 2022
ISBN: 978-1-941681-20-6
All rights reserved. Published by Burrow Press.
Limited first edition hardcovers available at: burrowpress.com

FIXED STARS

Marisa Siegel

Illustrations by Trisha Previte

BURROW PRESS | ORLANDO, FL

PRAISE FOR
FIXED STARS

"'Often it starts with a word,' writes Marisa Siegel near the beginning of *Fixed Stars*—and then she starts: sapphire, birdfeeders, everyone stuck with their own machines. The precision in these poems is remarkable, especially as Siegel pulls the language apart at its seams. What is rendered—absence, illness, motherhood, growing sweetgrass for a cat—is rendered by the buckling language, not in spite of it. Siegel writes, 'We form ourselves against particulars.' The field of the page nearly glows; *Fixed Stars* is incandescent."

—**KAVEH AKBAR** author of *Pilgrim Bell* and *Calling a Wolf a Wolf*

"These phenomenal poems ask us to enter the liminal space between seeing and saying, between the body and experience, between words and images. Marisa Siegel has given me fragments of a story I deeply recognize: the pieces of a self that exist in the interstices. In this work, the gaps and windows between sleep and sleeplessness, pleasure and pain, trauma and comfort, beauty and desire open their throats and to my wonder, there is song. There is soaring."

—**LIDIA YUKNAVITCH** author of *Verge* and *The Chronology of Water*

"In Marisa Siegel's Fixed Stars the language builds a home then carefully slips through its rooms. Patterns are drawn and patterns are broken. With image and word *Fixed Stars* flowers from darkness, radiates, bursts with color, as each section, each page, unfolds. Despite the palpable dangers these poems have made their way, have arrived like a gift from the rain."

—**ANDRÉS CERPA** author of *The Vault* and *Bicycle in a Ransacked City: An Elegy*

"Don't let the title fool you: there is nothing static about Marisa Siegel's *Fixed Stars*. Two words that come to mind are immediacy and dynamism, the poems themselves like the 'windows[s] of reinterpretation' she describes. Thanks to Trisha Previte's captivating artwork and the risks Siegel takes with syntax, punctuation, white space, and associative leaps, *Fixed Stars* is a beautiful, one-of-a-kind collection."

—**MAGGIE SMITH** author of *Goldenrod* and *Good Bones*

"These poems whisper in a quiet house, sharing secrets, bringing long and closely-held memories and wishes to light, encircling the home with a hard-won tenderness. A worn and worried past (path) is yielding slowly, carefully toward a future of the poet's own design. If there are dangers in lingering too long in the past, in indecision, or in uncertainty, they are risks that this clear-eyed speaker knows well and has considered from many angles. This is a voice clarifying itself toward lucidity and luminosity—a chime sounding crystalline and true in the wind."

—**MARY-KIM ARNOLD** author of *The Fish & The Dove* and *Litany for the Long Moment*

"In Marisa Siegel's meditative chapbook, *Fixed Stars*, the difficulties of coming into safety after a history of peril are manifest as an alarm in need of Xanax, a stuck-open drawer, a spinning begging ceiling fan. *Fixed Stars* bears a broad formal range, incorporating space-punctured prose poems, dexterous stanzas, and canny line breaks that carry us into the light and unfurl us. Along with Siegel's speaker, we form ourselves both toward and against the particulars of a forensic exploration—digging up and covering up, peering through windows, eventually hanging the birdfeeder of delight. As Siegel writes, 'pilgrimage for a disciple cannot / rebuild that road,' yet 'hope is the thing whose embers / smolder for years.' Let the smoldering of *Fixed Stars* glow a burning hope in you."

—**ALICIA MOUNTAIN** author of *Four in Hand* and *High Ground Coward*

ONE
Pressing

There is a red button should we call someone not flashing but positively sure of redness pressure exerts itself in infinite ways pushing to push feel it in tensed fingers only call in emergency not flashing but pressure to the way red becomes fire and fire becomes everything democratic words like eels and we are slipping sense danger palpable cutting through the red emanating from the button succumbing seems more than optional even preferable a triumph for gravity the emergence of red fiery flashing a democratic emergency an accident.

It starts with a word   how much begins   begs entrance   gains access   only a word   not necessarily chosen; we are careless   accidents happen   what it sounds like to hit one's head on twenty-seven wooden stairs   familiar, red-worn carpet   all the way down   but first there was   it is forgotten   this becomes acceptable   unremembering words one says.

The sky ticks blue   not a raindrop in sight   tongue sticking out, parched   dahlias are pink   fresh and glowing like a baby on the table   there is countertop   the beautiful inanimate progress   green / yellow / gold light   full   flickering on patterned wallpaper   the modern shining in the sunlight.

Full stop   dig in   to our roots   the mantle of our lives   there was a house   I imagined it   entirely   granite and marble   seasons are approximate   often July is hot   in the fire makes rubies   scientifically   sapphire from stone   it's all formula.

A pond / reflecting / koi swimming slipping through strands / of refraction cue shadow and its companion the pathology justifies nothing the disease has created a ceiling fan making circles the way it begged / a porch to stand and / turn approach a daisy chain of street signs and corners not contiguous children laughing in a park / a schoolyard / a lawn making circles a curbed conversation what is not a gift a laugh / an echo shaking a hallway / a sliding between / tear dropping down inevitably in so much as there was a remark / an obscured doorway contagious memory / diagnosis correct or asymptomatic and unresolving predetermined lines and causality.

If it happens in the day   not a dream   if you wake up   it is real   the sleeping is mechanism   release haphazardly   no control   vehicle   for each   I could never sleep in cars   I could never sleep on airplanes   these flights   leaps of subconscious   then eyes peering   at all angles   unclear   or clearer   in the dark   someone else is sleeping   the breathing   the jealous tension of accidentally sharing   these dark moments   of spitting out truth   overwhelms   keeps me awake   I keep me awake   let's avoid the reason   let's just say sometimes I used to sleep in hotel bathtubs   let's just say I used to stay awake in closets with books.

Firmly even tightly fixed in place packaged together bound and tethered she makes an involuntary jerking abruptly relocating everything take summary control ration space alleged body abandonment / forfeiture by the former occupant not to be strict or exacting but having a plan: set free the circle and relax one's grip.

She kept the cat in the bag all these years   only grew ugly and suffocated   got bored dragging it out   procession   scruff of the neck   she is sorry   tears do not   a martyr make.

TWO
Open Drawer

That which takes on a life of its own

Regarding data: what proof symbolizes, standardizes. Leave a letter alone in a box on a shelf for a decade, it could disintegrate.

The sun is persistent, necessary. When the source of life is the source of death we become inextricably complicated

>	and to grow
>	and to breathe
>	and to cast a shadow

the outline of which is a signal, or signifier, a constant reminder. It is unclear

>	if here she gets out.

A drawer is opened and closed, searched and destroyed.

If she could, she would shred the sunlight

                                                          and its shadow.

Bury the evidence, recover the letter, burn the box.

Disregard the filing cabinets, prove impossible the folders, erase the infinite pages.

A drawer is opened—

(Skeleton collector)

The bones were buried years ago / buried yesterday / were never really buried and now we dig

We are digging every day, and someone is sure we've dug deeper than the bones were buried but the bones are not there

The drawer is empty   it isn't a trick but it isn't an accident

She had a special brush   she thought if she brushed the bones and murmured her quiet prayer   she could give them the answers   she could collect her paycheck she could go home

But the bones are not there, and the brush   she'd had it in her hand just a moment ago / just yesterday / ten years ago   it's gone

(Fossil recorder)

The moon as giant tape recorder   the moon as preserver of evidence, internal and external   the moon as recording signals   distinctive changes carved on rock

Even on the moon there is language

If not covered up   the recorded signal is overwritten and destroyed by later events: the coverage of old material by younger material

The moon tries to protect the signal   to preserve the fossil   to develop other processes

The moon, too, buries the record

The result of this coverage is to remove surface material from further processing   from wear and tear   from the inevitable subsequent impacts that will disperse   the buried material

(Jesus figure)

In the beginning there was stumbling   was gasp   was need to believe

We walked around the square blocks again and again and again
Is that when the circling began   I think it began then and had already been

Even in the beginning there was foxhole   was patch   was need for air

Trash bins knocked over   knocked around, and garbage strewn
That's when it became windy   became messy   bits of wreckage in her hair

(Father figure)

The scene refuses to be set

There might've been a moment when she could have climbed out but the window was locked   or there was no window

Not afraid of heights not afraid of climbing not really sure what to be afraid of so the answer is everything

Search through the records of sleeping   the ratio of dream to nightmare

Last night in a dream I killed you   early this morning I killed you   the desperation shaking the air in waves

Set the scene in the bedroom   and the bedroom disappears

Never trust what you can't see

A room without an emergency exit. Voices hushed. Dim bulbs flicker, make shadows sing across a low ceiling. We stare at the black void of a floor we hope is underfoot.

I am leaving these things I will not say goodbye to for years.

I am putting this conversation on ice.

It will scab over, this moment before I leave.

Look:

two cigarettes, lit briefly, put out. Parallel on the asphalt; suggesting something sinister, or

people tired of each other's company.

Late Afternoon

This that loves spider
that hangs web, caught raindrop

This that loves order
against corner and what gathers there

We hang a birdfeeder
for the children
and the birds

(and the child we are)
(and the bird we are)

Inventory

Spelling in shorthand indicates the lack of sincerity behind the sentiment;
shouldn't we call that card by its name?

No way to avoid this aging—
no hiding in the other to avoid turning.

Jealous is so uncomplicated / life is really complicated.

Is that shorthand?

What I mean is: turn the gaze inward—any honest indication
of sentiment is unexpected; any indication of progression is unlikely.

The drawer will not close—

Perspective

That didn't involve formula. That wasn't about circumstance. That isn't context. That is forgotten. That is eventuality. That finds beginning. That we'll give—ours is temporary. That didn't catch. That promise we didn't. That word caught in throat. That finally, forgive. That is understood and that is mistaken.

That looses her circumstance. That forgets formula. That shrugs context. That remembers: movement. That is unwritten. That is divergence, a couplet. That searches always. That we'll break—ours is captivating. That stuck. That returns, or rises. That evenly split and that jagged edge.

That formulates circumstance. Contextual movement. Ours is scientific. That undone button. That unlit fact.

Ours is reduced. That disappeared rim. Disappointed sun.

Not-Index

abrade	canyon	gravity	proof
alarm	cat	her(e)	relation
angle	circle/-ing	hoof-taps	river
awake	clocks	illegible	root(ed)
axes	coincidence	implicit	rubies
basement	corner	indefatigable	science
bedrock	dig/-ging	investigation	shoreline
bedroom	dis-ease	island	shoulder(ed)
bench	drawer	July	story
bird	dream	lake	structure
birthday	dumpster	lighthouse	stuck
blood	echoes	line(s)	sun(light)
boardwalk	evidence	magic trick	swing
bones	explanation	marked	symmetry
boundary	fence	math	(t)here
box(es)	fix(ed)	mineral	water
boxcutter	force(d)	mirror	weedy
buried	gate	moon	window
calendar	ghost(s)	nightmare	yielding
California	gold	ocean	you

THREE
Particulars

-ning / begin

When the cat dropped
dead on the living
room rug time shifted.

Hope is the thing
whose embers
smolder for years—

a decade, longer.

I see her shadow across
my living days, her quiet
and small softness.

Ways we avoid the future

At a party, pick up a bench and throw it straight at the consequences.

Don't watch the car hit the roadblock. Don't wonder that you aren't troubled by clanging danger. Continue resting your head in the familiar lap of broken.

Sleep for two years, wake up to feed the cat, delay the inevitable.

Ask how she places emphasis skillfully, listen to the sounds of an answer. Study as he cultivates an attractive standoffishness.

Practice, practice,

practice. Leave halfway through the movie. Pull up roots quicker than they push down. Weed the yard, leave every home you tend to.

Collect excuses, build a careful museum to house your collection.

Notes: windows (setting the scene)

Theoretical window cracks open. Windows actual and imaginary, practically glass and problematic in transparency.

The drama of window and its associated ornamentation.

Specific window made up of intersecting lines,
pattern of twos repeating.

Window out green lawn, bench and tree—
Sleeping basement window—
Stained-glass library window—
Bougainvillea bedroom window—

We don't see through windows so much as imagine what we might see through windows.

Who climbing in window and who climbing out window.

Which window
which occasion
was it daytime or was it
middle-of-night
did you knock or
just leave?

Window: word with significance.

Porch window, watching fist shatter. A window both
actual and theoretical, such that we are always discussing its implications.

Another window on set.
If there are words to open this window I will:
a window neither opened nor closed
a logic not exactly of a window but of a crack
in a foundation, tangle of roots.

If you're this far down to the bumbling mistake you'll see the possibility of window
distracts. I am afraid it will be perpetual window. Too many windows to set only one
scene.

By design

About fences and gates: it's the swing. Constant accompaniment of memory taking form, herded through other memories—of many memories at once. Complement of concordant shapes.

Preemptive protection. Boundary-defining safety but built to be difficult, presumptuously defensive in stature. Disappearing; throwing the blame over. Shifting.

The constant circling, tensed shoulders ready, the linear ignorance of certain gesture, refusal to look back. Decision: a made and folded thing.

Home is where

       , and continues to manage—
       all that blood in and out
       a constant
               the pumping and fluctuation

Valves as doors
          were there walls
              and would they impede
              your fine health
or situate, give context
which is necessary

a situation,
in context,
drains of blood,
refills

to be alive the heart lives
                            and inside a body
        but that body, it doesn't
        need walls, necessarily

the machine deliberates, keeps you
                            breathing and thinking
                            moving
                            in   and through   the room

settles, like water
        settles—
        it must settle,
        somewhere.

For those who encompass worlds:

This poem is a secret — is tarnished with the habit of discretion

the value in counting reaches
past limit —

given a prescribed boundary, make shelter in number

two:
        phrases overlap
        eliding not omitting,

                                    allowing for difficulty

a window of reinterpretation.

Control

My son wants to know
why I can't control the rain, *Mama*
he says earnestly, *is a boss*.
I feel responsible, as though
I've brought rain and sky
and all the world's trouble
into our safe blue kitchen.

My sister texts a photo
of me, near in age to my son.
I see me but also him
and I am terrified, I know
since before I can remember

I have brought rain and sky
into other kitchens and only
myself, my unstable body
keeps my son safe and dry

in our blue kitchen
as we stare at a photo
of me but also of him.

Since before I can remember,
all the world's trouble, a baby
girl in a photo responsible
for keeping safe a body.
Took control, spurned the rain
harnessed the sky, broke
the sunlight. Walks away.

Three

1. You

exist in ink. This was promised
my silence. Strange kind of redemption:
I will never be strong enough
for all I can't know to protect
from what I've tied up in you.

Pilgrimage for a disciple cannot
rebuild that road and thusly wanders.

I am plagued.

2. And you

exist, I have let you be.
It is purposeful, keeps you safe.
Late at night a painting forms a couch,
a catch. For that once-

holy conversation
when you asked
if you could
I will not separate you
out or mention forgiveness.

We know I pretend, you and I
have seen the howling bottoms of it.

3. But you

exist in my bones. How many versions made
convenient mirrors to distract. How I grew
used to your inhabitance. How I used you.

You do not deserve this company I allow
you to keep. Poor arbiter I remain
indoctrinated not fully but full, echo
off a tinny roof and summer rain.
Cure the nightmare

I am waiting.

The problem

The problem is a question
of course. A defined shape,

often a circle.

The question is the problem, also
this is not math class. Obviously

there's resistance.

No one is being witty, everyone
has their own machines.

Every bug an infestation

Here is a bee, and a death.
When he coughs she can't
breath. The alarm
needs a battery and why
wouldn't history   repeating
myself.

My sleep is broken, she
said   the day   she woke up.

A pink castle   behind glass;
she never broke
code— only window—
and later, foot,
promise, perhaps.
This isn't her
confession,

this dream   is recurring, she
knows but if   she could sleep.

Here: a thief, a friend.
He smiles   she can't
breath   her alarm
needs a Xanax and why
wouldn't history   judging
myself.

Her number   is up, she
knew   the heart   is a gate.

Black shirt   cutting shears;
it might have been that
lie— only a photograph,
and later, a feeling   a prayer,
perhaps   this isn't   her
confession.

He had a key   she
wouldn't   have   locked the door.

Tugging at the edges

Last spring I grew sweet grass for the cat.
As sprouts shot up and bent toward the slivers of sunlight coming through the slats I
pulled one seed from the soil and considered: roots firm to the earth, green up in the air.

I tug at the worn edges of metaphor.
The chrysalis begins to split, slowly opens to allow the new spring limbs
                                                        a space
                                                      to unfurl in the world.

with sunlight / Forgiveness

is a word for replacing not to replace but substitute
a branch to stand the proud fence straight up / down

road as invitation as impassible / impossible to pass
up and down the myth of improbability that was

words as fences / are fences not as cages but question
the whole idea of cages and / as closure is impossible

it comes to pass: we replace past transgressions
with / in a calculated time, an invitation marked date

becomes myth held down and drawn out perhaps not
straight or involving lines replacing circles

im / possible to break out of so back to borders back
to time-frames / calendar and roots out a solution

Particulars

We form ourselves against particulars:

that tree
that square of grass
that swing

Tied to you now
even if far from
as to desert
low and dry heat, no snow

There was a bench, tree dipped
down and you pulled a leaf
pulled words
stretched
yourself

We form toward particulars:

weeping willow
quadrangle
pergola

There was couch, a painting
a story you told
yourself

What walls can contain:
the breathing
and the wide hallways

each necessary to each.

ABOUT THE AUTHOR & ARTIST

Marisa Siegel holds an MFA in Poetry from Mills College in Oakland, CA. Her essay "Inherited Anger" appears in the anthology *Burn It Down*, edited by Lilly Dancyger (Seal Press, 2019).

Trisha Previte is an illustrator, designer, and explorer hailing from Cleveland, Ohio and based in New York City. She received her BFA in Fine Arts from the Stamps School of Art & Design at the University of Michigan, with a minor in Environmental Studies.

www.ingramcontent.com/pod-product-compliance
Lightning Source LLC
Chambersburg PA
CBHW051808100526
44592CB00016B/2620